SEO Basics

How to use Search Engine Optimization to take your Business to the next level of Success

Table of Contents

INTRODUCTION 1

CHAPTER 1 – WHAT IS SEARCH ENGINE OPTIMIZATION AND HOW CAN YOU USE IT? 3

    THE STANDARD DEFINITION FOR SEARCH ENGINE OPTIMIZATION 4

CHAPTER 2 – HOW SEARCH ENGINES WORK 7

    WEB CRAWLING AND INDEXING 8
    DIFFERENCE BETWEEN SEARCH ENGINES & WEB DIRECTORIES 9
    STOP WORDS 10
    TERM STEMMING 10
    INDEX ENTRY EXTRACTION 10
    THE WORKING OF A SEARCH ENGINE 11
    PAGE AUTHORITY 11
    CONTENT 12
    LINKS 12

CHAPTER 3 – DIFFERENT TYPES OF SEARCH ENGINE OPTIMIZATION 13

    BLACK HAT SEO 14
    HOW TO AVOID BLACK HAT SEO 14
    KEY WORD STUFFING 15
    DOORWAY PAGES 15
    INVISIBLE TEXT 15
    WHITE HAT SEO 16

CHAPTER 4 – HOW TO OPTIMIZE YOUR WEBSITE/PAGE FOR SEARCH ENGINES 18

CHAPTER 5 – KEEPING UP WITH SEO 24

CHAPTER 6 – SEARCH ENGINE OPTIMIZATION AND RANKING TIPS 30

CHAPTER 7 – SEO IN A NUTSHELL 34

CONCLUSION 37

Introduction

I want to thank you and congratulate you for downloading the book, SEO Basics.

This book contains proven steps and strategies on how to use search engine Optimization to make your business a huge success.

This book introduces the readers to the world of SEO in the simplest of terms. SEO can be difficult to understand, but in this book everything from A-Z is covered. It explains what Search Engine Optimization is, why it is important, how search engines work, how to optimize a page or a website for a search engine, different types of SEO techniques, along with various tips and tricks to reap long-term benefits.

Thanks again for downloading this book, I hope you enjoy it!

Chapter 1 – What is Search Engine Optimization and how can you use it?

No matter what you do online, at one point or another, you will come across the word 'SEO.' Search Engine Optimization. So, what is this search engine Optimization? Why is there so much hype about it? Why does it matter, and what can it do for you? Why is it so important?

If you make a new website or a blog, a part of the process will be optimising it for search engines.

The standard definition for Search Engine Optimization **is:**

"Search Engine Optimization (SEO) is the process of affecting the visibility of a website in a search engine's 'natural' or 'organic' search results."

A few years ago, I made a website, and ignored the step where I could optimize it for search engines. I did not think I needed it. A year later, the average traffic per day on my website was somewhere between 5 and 9. My website was really well made. I made everything clear, from what it was all about to the services I offered. The website failed because I skipped one of the most important things. I didn't optimize it for search engines.

Search Engine Optimization is what you do to bring more traffic to your website. When you search for something on a search engine, like Google, the results you see are search engine optimized. Optimising your website for a search engine improves its visibility. It makes it easy for the search engines to find it, and for the people to find your website, page, or business. The most well-optimized websites are on the front page. Most people never look beyond the first three pages on a search engine. When you search for something, you get tens of pages with results. If your website is somewhere in the middle or the end, the odds of anyone finding your website are pretty slim. That is precisely why you need to optimize your website for search engines, and bring it to the front page.

The results you see on your search engines are primarily of two types:

- Paid
- Unpaid

The paid and sponsored results are highlighted and stand apart from others. For these, people have to pay to the search engine. There are charges associated with every click so it can be very, very expensive. Therefore, we focus on generating natural or organic traffic.

Search engines have algorithms and web crawlers that help them filter the websites so the results can be authentic and free of spam. The more authentic a website looks to the search engine, the higher it will rank.

In the next chapters, we will discuss the methods and strategies that will help you optimize your website or content for search engines to rank higher in the results, and to bring more traffic to your website. We will also discuss the different types of SEO, the difference between them, and how to ensure that your website gets indexed. I will also make sure to explain everything in the simplest words possible so you can fully grasp the concepts.

Chapter 2 – How Search Engines Work

A search engine is basically a program. When you search for something using this program, it uses the words you type and searches its database, matches your queries in its index, and brings you the most relevant results. There are algorithms involved in almost every step that ensure that the results you get are the most relevant.

In order to understand search engine Optimization, you need to understand how search engines work. We will start with crawling and indexing.

Web Crawling and Indexing

A web crawler is either a program or a script used by search engines. The crawler used by Google is called 'Googlebot,' and is the most popular web crawler today. The job of a crawler is to browse all the websites on the internet that are available publicly. It creates copies of the content it browses on the websites, to be processed by the search engine later onwards. They also help the search engines to keep their data up to date.

A search engine will eventually add your website to its database; you can also do it manually. When the search engine has discovered the URL to your website, or added it to its database, it will schedule it for crawling. There are several different factors involved here, and the list of websites is rearranged by an algorithm. Not all the websites that are in the database are crawled.

After the crawling comes the indexing. During indexing, which is also determined by an algorithm, words related to your document point to it. That is when you can say that your website has been indexed, or added to the search engine's index. Remember, search engines have algorithms that decide whether or not to crawl or index pages.

Difference between Search Engines & Web Directories

Although the terms are often used interchangeably, search engines and web directories are not the same.

A search engine creates the list or index of websites automatically. Web crawlers keep the content on the search engines up to date.

A web directory is usually an organised list of websites. Unlike search engines, it is maintained and updated by human beings, not web crawlers. While they may not be as comprehensive as search engines, the websites they list are usually free of spam. It is hard to trick them because the lists are maintained and updated by humans, not automated scripts.

Stop Words

When the entries are being indexed, the search engines delete the stop words. Stop words include words like: he, she, it, a, and, the, is, are, etc. that are of no use in terms of search. As a result, the search becomes much more efficient, quick, and fast. In the past, this was important because memory was expensive. Now, even though the memory is cheap, time and speed matter a lot more than they used to. So, to expedite the search process, the stop words are deleted.

Term Stemming

During this step, the suffixes are removed. This is also to speed up the searching process. For example, the system will look at the page and find similar words, like: forge, forged, forging, forgery, etc. What it will do is index the term 'forg' instead of indexing all the similar terms.

Index Entry Extraction

After term stemming, the index entries are extracted and a shortened version of the page is stored. It looks less like the original page and probably does not make any sense if it is read, but it is never presented for reading. The resulting page only makes the searching of entries easier by removing the irrelevant entries.

The Working of a Search Engine

There are many different search engines available today, and all of them work in different ways. There are some basic steps that are followed by all search engines, although they constantly update their search methods. For instance, Amazon has its own search engine, and while it is mostly the same as other search engines, it has one key difference: it uses categories. But this is just to give you an idea of how search engines differ from each other. Our main focus is on search engines like Google, Yahoo, Bing, etc. where you can get your website listed, indexed, and ranked higher.

Then comes the searching and matching. When you search for a term, the search engine will look for it in its indexes, match the term, and bring forth the results.

Page Authority

The pages are also ranked depending on their authority. Authority pages get the top rankings, so you have to ensure that you make authority pages. The authority of a page depends on two things:

Content

Links

Content

This is the stuff that you write on the page. It includes key words and is crawled by the web crawler.

Links

Links tell the search engine that your page is important. If different websites or pages link to your page, the search engine will realise the importance of your page. The more links you have, the more authority your page will get. You can think of these links as votes; votes that will help you rank higher in the results. The more votes you get, the higher you will rank.

Now, to make your business successful, you have two goals:

1. Keep writing content with the right key words to promote your page and make it easier for it to be found.

2. Try and build links to rank higher in the search results and build more authority for your page.

Doing the things mentioned above is called Search Engine Optimization. In the next chapter, we will discuss the different types of SEO.

Chapter 3 – Different Types of Search Engine Optimization

As with all other things, there are two ways in which a page can be optimized for a search engine. They are:

Black Hat SEO

White Hat SEO

Black Hat SEO

Black Hat search engine Optimization is the unethical way. It is not recommended, but it is important to understand it so that you know what to avoid when optimising your page for a search engine. Black Hat SEO is basically the abuse of tactics, techniques, and strategies of White Hat SEO. The techniques are used aggressively to rank higher in the search engines. Search engines have their own rules and guidelines, which are not followed or obeyed in Black Hat SEO. The pages are filled with key words, also called 'keyword stuffing,' doorway pages are added, content that is actually irrelevant and misleading is used, etc. But the results of Black Hat SEO are only short term, and the websites that do this end up getting banned by the search engines and are removed from their lists. Black Hat SEO does not bring any long-term benefits.

How to Avoid Black Hat SEO

Here's how to avoid Black Hat SEO:

Key Word Stuffing

Filling your pages only with keywords with the goal to rank higher in the search engine's results may help you rank higher quickly, but will eventually get you banned by the search engine. So, avoid stuffing your page with key words.

Doorway Pages

This is another way to abuse SEO. A fake page is created that tricks the web crawlers and results in the website ranking higher, although this page is invisible to the users. For long-term success, your goal should be to create a quality and valuable website that improves the experience for the users. Do not create any doorway pages.

Invisible Text

Long lists of keywords are added on the pages to trick the crawlers. The colour of the text is kept the same as the background of the page so the text remains invisible unless highlighted by the user. This is another unethical technique that should never be used.

White Hat SEO

White Hat SEO is the ethical SEO. When you use the techniques, tactics, and strategies of SEO as you are supposed to, and, as regulated by the search engines, then that is called White Hat Search Engine Optimization. It involves the use of key words, building links, backlinking, keyword analysis, etc. It results in long-term benefits because the authority of your pages continues to be strengthened, and there is no risk of your page getting banned by the search engines.

In the next chapter we will discuss how to optimize your page for a search engine using the White Hat Search Engine Optimization techniques.

Chapter 4 – How to Optimize your Website/Page for Search Engines

Let's jump right into Search Engine Optimization!

Keywords

Keywords are the words that people type on search engines to search for something. During Search and Match, the keywords of the user are matched with the content on your website, so it is very important to make sure that you have the right keywords on your page. But how do you choose the right SEO keywords?

Do not be too generic

The keywords that you use on your page should not be too generic. If they are too generic, your page will get lost in the results. People looking for it will not find it easily, and the ranking will go down. If your business is about a shampoo, then the keyword 'business,' or 'hair,' will be too generic. The word business will result in different businesses, and the term hair will lead to hundreds of pages about hair. If your website is about an herbal shampoo that is for volumizing hair for women, then your keywords would 'volumizing,' 'hair,' 'shampoo,' and 'herbal.' These keywords increase the scope.

Do not be too specific

Do not be too specific with your keywords either. Your goal is to increase the overall scope while staying on the topic. If your keywords are 'how to,' or similar, then websites like Wikihow and HowThingsWork will take the lead, and your website will be lost in the results. The keywords need to be balanced so while the scope is broad, the results still lead to your website.

Be Consistent

The process of ranking higher in search results takes time. The keywords you use should be consistent with what your website is about. You have to stay focused and approach the same thing in different ways. The keywords should not be about something that you focus on once in a while only. If your keywords are focussed on what you do regularly, are consistent, then voila! Your website will rank higher! Whatever your website focuses on, whatever your keywords are, write about them as often as you can.

Titles, Subtitles, and Descriptions

Do not keep the keywords limited to the general writing. The titles should always include a keyword or two. Keep the titles short but make sure that there is a sprinkling of keywords in them. Ideally, a title should be between 10-14 words, and should start with a keyword.

Subtitles can also be utilised for keywords. You can use more keywords in the subtitles.

The description is where the rest of the content is. An ideal density of keywords is said to be 1%, which means that there should ideally be at least one keyword in every 100 words of description or content. For better search engine Optimization, make sure that the keywords are used in the first 3 lines, or the introductory lines, of the page.

Keyword Research

Before you start using keywords, you should do some keyword research. It gives you an idea about the relevant terms that people search for, so you know what people search for when looking for something, and then use those keywords to help them find your page or website. For example, when you are typing something in a search engine like Google, you will notice that the search engine also suggests something before you have even finished typing. At least half of the time, what you are searching for shows up. Google calls it Google Suggest. You can also use Google Insight or Adwords Keyword Estimator to get an idea about the keywords that people search for. In Black Hat SEO, people just research and find out the keywords that people search for and stuff their pages with them, but the same technique of researching can be used in an ethical way and for your own benefit. You can include this in your research to learn more about how people look for things, what terms they type, when looking for a business like yours, and then include them in your keywords. Because the end goal here is that the user should be able to find your website or page.

URLS

The URL of your website or the specific page should also include the keywords.

Build Links

Finally, try to build links. Get similar and relevant websites to link back to your website or pages. If the content on your website is good enough, people will automatically link back to it. If you write a good article on giving a back massage, someone writing about getting rid of back pain and suggesting massage may link back to your page. Similarly, if you offer a good hair product, a website that contains information about hair may link back to your page to let people know that the product you offer is good. Alternatively, you can bring attention to your page. You can ask people to link back to your page, not only for building links but also to help others. A good linking techniques used by websites is offering discounts. For instance, website B shows a link to website A along with a 5% discount offer, which makes the people on the website B go to website A. Social media also helps by playing a vital role in this. People share and re-share good content and offers, and this also helps build links.

Chapter 5 – Keeping Up with SEO

Search Engine Optimization is not a one-time thing but an ongoing process. To continue to rank higher, you need to continue to produce good content to stay in the limelight of the search engines.

Have a Blog

Blogs are places for writing, no matter what you write about. You can write daily, weekly, or monthly on a blog. Search engines keep their data updated, and also note how frequently a page or website is updated. So, try to get new content on your website, page, or blog at least 5 times a week. All this content should also be search engine optimized.

Plan Ahead of Time

Don't just take it as it comes. Have everything planned ahead of time. This gives you time to build upon and improve your content. It ensures that you are consistent.

Stay Up to Date

Keep yourself updated with what's going on in the world. If your website is based on mental illnesses, then keep up with the world of mental illnesses. Find out what research is being done on it, shed your light on new research, and throw in your two cents. As soon as the word spreads about something new, people seeking answers search for it. Your goal is to make sure that the right people find your website too, and that they get to see what you have to say about it and what you have shared.

Give Them Something More

If your website is an online business, not every post should be about selling stuff. If you are always trying to sell something, if you are always focusing your articles on what you sell, people might be put off and get the feeling that they are being forced or cornered. So, if your website sells a volumising hair shampoo, it is better to just write about hair problems like hair dryness to bring them to your website. If they do visit your website, they will browse around.

Give Them Something of Value

If you write with the goal of getting people on your website without providing value, there will be no benefits. Search engines also notice how much time a user spends on a page or website. If the users leave quickly, your page gets down voted. So you have to provide content that is valuable. It should be good enough that people give it their time, actually stop and read or browse around. The more time they spend on your website, the better.

Linking Back

It is quite the opposite of backlinking, but the results are similar. Link back to good websites and pages. Search engines already know about the good and authentic pages, and when they see that your website is sending people to those pages, they up vote your website because they realise that your website is giving the users more quality. The focus here is on 'quality,' so make sure that you don't just link back, but link back to quality websites, or it can be counter-productive.

Add Photos

Most people have short attention spans, so having photos on the websites can help retain their attention for a while longer. In addition, photos relevant to the content increase the overall visual appeal of the page. People, today, have short attention spans, more so on the internet. This gives you a very little time to capture their attention, so you have to do all you can to make them stay. When adding a photo, rename it and use a keyword in the name.

Keep It Interesting

Do not bore the visitors. Whatever content you put on your website, keep it relevant and interesting by using interesting headlines, catchy titles, and brief descriptions.

Word Count

Most search engines ignore the pages that have less than 500 words. Whatever you write about should contain at least 500 words so that the search engines and crawlers take it into account.

Meta Data

The Meta data contains information about what your page includes. Most website hosts have made it easier for the clients today and removed the manual work, so all you need to do is ensure that the meta data also contains the keywords that are appropriate and relevant to the information offered on the page.

Use Categories

This is mostly for blogs. The blogs can touch on a variety of subjects, so instead of having a huge unsorted archive, use categories and sort out all the data. It makes it easier for the users and visitors, and also gets you noticed by the search engines.

Chapter 6 – Search Engine Optimization and Ranking Tips

Here are some important tips that will help you improve the Optimization of your page and rank higher.

Readability

The content you write on your website should be readable. It should engage the visitors. It should sound like a human wrote it, not a robot. Robotic tones make people lose interest and result in them bouncing off your page, which harms the rankings. Readability takes several things into account, including grammar, formatting, and tone.

Grammar:

When the content is grammatically incorrect, it offends the readers. When it is grammatically correct, it is more readable.

Formatting:

The content should be properly formatted. Do not use colours that blend into the background, or are so bright or light that it is difficult to read them. For instance, it is very difficult to read text that has the colour 'lime' on a white background. Use headings, subheadings, paragraphs, and bullets to make things easier on the eyes.

Tone:

The tone should be maintained properly, be it professional or conversational. The conversational tone is more engaging, but the tone you need to use depends on where it is being used.

Again, in short, write like human beings write.

Do not change the domain name of your website

One of the factors in the ranking of your website is its domain name. The older the domain name, the more authentic it is. So do not change your domain name every often or throw away a good one. In addition, changing your domain name too often also results in loss of visitors.

Get your website indexed

If your website is not indexed, you can do it manually; and it is completely free. Following are the links to the popular search engines where you can submit your website:

Google: http://www.google.com/submityourcontent/

Yahoo: http://search.yahoo.com/info/submit.html

Bing: http://www.bing.com/toolbox/submit-site-url

Keep your website active

Search engines use crawlers to keep their content up to date. If you do not update often, or at all, the crawler will have nothing to report for it. The search engines want to keep their databases up to date, and that is an opportunity for you to improve your rankings as well, because by updating frequently, the message you send to the search engines is that your website is active, alive, and kicking.

Load Times

Only keep the relevant data on your website. Too many photos, animated images, gadgets, effects, etc. slow down the loading time of the page, so to make sure that your page loads faster, remove anything and everything that is not essential to it. Sort everything out and put things in relevant places, so that the website loads faster. The less content it has to load, the faster it will be. Websites with too much non-essential content do not load properly or completely on slower connections.

Focus

Stay focused! The website should focus on one main thing and stay focussed on it. It can branch from there on, have secondary topics, but it should never lose focus of the primary thing it is about.

Chapter 7 – SEO in a Nutshell

Here's a quick run through search engine Optimization from the beginning to end.

- You begin by finding out who your audience is. Once you have identified your audience, you have to find out that what do they search for when they need products or services that you offer.

- There are databases on the internet that have this information. They help you find out what people looking for your products or services search for. This is a part of the keyword research, and does not infringe on anyone's privacy, because the only information they provide is what your audience searches for, nothing personal about them.

- Then come the common phrases that people search for. They are common, hence, when used, they will bring organic traffic to your website.

- But, it is important to also find out other similar websites who use the same keywords. Know your enemies, or competition. You have to know who you are up against to beat them.

- Keywords! Keywords are the words that people use in the searches, words that you can get from online databases, Google Insight, etc. to bring your audience to your website.

- Links are votes of authenticity. Authenticity brings you to the top of the rankings. So, you have to get other websites to link back to you to increase the authenticity of your pages, and you have to link back to quality pages to let the search engine know that your website focuses on and provides quality.

- Content: It includes everything that is on your website. It should be well-written, formatted, and must contain keywords. No matter how good all the content is, if it does not have the keywords, people will not find it. If people do not find it, you do not get any visitors and the ranking goes down.

- Engage and Capture the Interest: Whatever content you put on your website, it should be interesting and engage your visitors.

- Blogs: blogs are perfect for search engine Optimization. A website can be limiting in terms of content, but that's where the blogs come in. A website can only contain so much content, but a blog is all about content. You can update a blog frequently, and if it is a part of your website, your website will benefit from it too.

- Consistency and Focus: Lastly, consistency and focus are important. You should keep everything consistent, stay focused, and not lose track of what your website primarily is about.

- Be Patient! Search engines take their time. If you want to reap long-term benefits, you will have to be persistent and patient.

Conclusion

Thank you again for downloading this book!

I hope this book was able to help you understand and learn search engine Optimization.

The next step is to start optimising your pages for search engines and start generating organic traffic.

Finally, if you enjoyed this book, then I'd like to ask you for a favor, would you be kind enough to leave a review for this book on Amazon? It'd be greatly appreciated!

[Click here to leave a review for this book on Amazon!](http://amzn.to/1tapef0)

http://amzn.to/1tapef0

Thank you and good luck!

Check Out My Other Books

Below you'll find some of my other popular books that are popular on Amazon and Kindle as well. Simply click on the links below to check them out.

[SEO Basics: How to use Search Engine Optimization (SEO) to take your business to the next level of success](#)

[Social Media Marketing for Beginners: How to build a social media strategy that really works](#)

[Affiliate Marketing for Beginners: Simple, smart and proven strategies to make A LOT of money online, the easy way](#)

If the links do not work, for whatever reason, you can simply search for these titles on the Amazon website to find them.

© Copyright 2014 - All rights reserved.

This document is geared towards providing exact and reliable information in regards to the topic and issue covered. The publication is sold with the idea that the publisher is not required to render accounting, officially permitted, or otherwise, qualified services. If advice is necessary, legal or professional, a practiced individual in the profession should be ordered.

- From a Declaration of Principles which was accepted and approved equally by a Committee of the American Bar Association and a Committee of Publishers and Associations.

In no way is it legal to reproduce, duplicate, or transmit any part of this document in either electronic means or in printed format. Recording of this publication is strictly prohibited and any storage of this document is not allowed unless with written permission from the publisher. All rights reserved.

The information provided herein is stated to be truthful and consistent, in that any liability, in terms of inattention or otherwise, by any usage or abuse of any policies, processes, or directions contained within is the solitary and utter responsibility of the recipient reader. Under no circumstances will any legal responsibility or blame be held against the publisher for any reparation, damages, or monetary loss due to the information herein, either directly or indirectly.

Respective authors own all copyrights not held by the publisher.

The information herein is offered for informational purposes solely, and is universal as so. The presentation of the information is without contract or any type of guarantee assurance.

The trademarks that are used are without any consent, and the publication of the trademark is without permission or backing by the trademark owner. All trademarks and brands within this book are for clarifying purposes only and are the owned by the owners themselves, not affiliated with this document.

www.ingramcontent.com/pod-product-compliance
Lightning Source LLC
Chambersburg PA
CBHW051823170526
45167CB00005B/2135